"I take your hand in mine . . ."

OTHER WORKS BY CAROL ROCAMORA

Chekhov: Four Plays

Chekhov: The Early Plays

Chekhov's Vaudevilles

If you require pre-publication information about upcoming Smith and Kraus books, you may receive our semiannual catalogue, free of charge, by sending your name and address to *Smith and Kraus Catalogue, P.O. Box 127, Lyme, NH 03768. Or call us at (603) 643-6431. www.SmithandKraus.com*

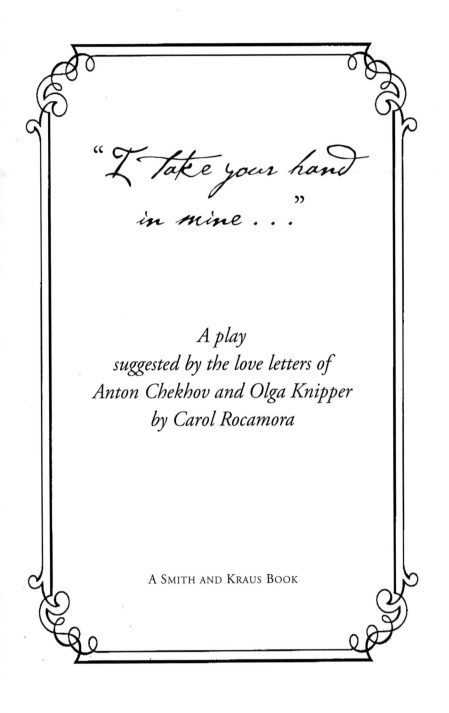

"I take your hand in mine . . ."

A play
suggested by the love letters of
Anton Chekhov and Olga Knipper
by Carol Rocamora

A SMITH AND KRAUS BOOK

A Smith and Kraus Book
Published by Smith and Kraus, Inc.
177 Lyme Road, Hanover, New Hampshire 03755
www.SmithandKraus.com

Cover and Text Design by Julia Hill Gignoux, Freedom Hill Design
Photos courtsey of the State Museum of Literature, Chekhov Museum, Moscow

First Edition: November 2000
9 8 7 6 5 4 3 2 1

The Library of Congress Cataloging-In-Publication Data

Rocamora, Carol.
"I take your hand in mine—" : a new play / by Carol Rocamora. —1st ed.
p. cm.
"Based on the love letters of Anton Chekhov and Olga Knipper."
ISBN 1-57525-244-9 / ISBN-13 978-1-57525-244-5
1. Chekhov, Anton Pavlovich, 1860–1904—Drama. 2. Knipper-Chekhova, Olga Leonardovna, 1868–1959—Drama. 3. Authors' spouses—Drama. 4. Authors—Drama. 5. Russia—Drama. I. Title.

PS3568.O3213 I15 2000
812'.54—dc21 00-050985

Introduction

A few winters ago, Olympia Dukakis, that marvelous American actress, gave me an idea. Like me, she treasures the plays of the great Russian writer, Anton Chekhov. And, like me, she has always been very moved by the love story of the playwright and Olga Knipper, actress of the Moscow Art Theatre. So she suggested I write a play about it. "For Louis and me," she said. (She and her fine actor-husband, Louis Zorich, have a lifelong relationship with Chekhov's major plays. They have appeared in virtually all of them at the Williamstown Theatre Festival, during the Nikos Psacharopoulus years. And each of them has directed a number of them, too.)

So I wrote a play. And Olympia and Louis read it to my students at New York University's Tisch School of the Arts this fall. They were wonderful. And now Marisa Smith and Eric Kraus, also devotés of Chekhov, have published it.

Everybody loves a love story. But this one is special. Special, because it's one about two extraordinary people in extraordinary circumstances. He, a great playwright and humanitarian, who knew his life would be brief. She, a great actress and founding leading lady of one of the world's most famous theater companies, who was full of vitality and passion. When they met, he was thirty-eight; she was twenty-nine. They knew each other only six years; they were married for three of them, until his death in July, 1904. (It was the first marriage for each. She lived till ninety-one, and never remarried.) During those six short years, circumstances — his health, her work — kept them apart almost all that time. He was banished to Yalta for medical reasons; she, committed to Moscow for the theater season. And though they were together during the summer, his ever-declining health marred the quality of that precious time.

And yet it is through these circumstances that their moving love story is told. For they wrote each other letters — roughly 400 each —

during that six-year period when they were mostly apart. Passionate, open, spontaneous letters. The letters were full of longing and love and humor, full of the rich detail of their everyday lives, as artists and ordinary people. These details provide the tapestry for a theatrical "portrait of a marriage."

So the story of their love can be told in their own voices. And I have attempted to do just that. In this effort, I am indebted to the fine scholarship of Jean Benedetti, whose translations of their selected correspondence, entitled *Dear Writer, Dear Actress,* pointed the way for me to a number of these letters, in addition to the ones I already knew, as well as to her memoirs. I have myself, of course, retranslated all those letters and reminiscences anew from the original Russian, to mold this little play. I call it "*I take your hand in mine . . .*" his way of signing his letters to her during the early months of their correspondence.* And I have occasionally taken "liberties" with the original letters, excerpting them, and, in a few instances, adding dialogue to fill a gap where there is no correspondence — all toward the goal of helping to tell the story dramatically.

In addition, I have tried to incorporate illuminating biographical detail into the play, for the benefit of those readers and audience members who may be less familiar with the lives of Anton Chekhov and Olga Knipper than we theater folk are. I've also tried to highlight the connections between their personal lives and his writing, to illustrate how Chekhov took material from this relationship for his last two major plays. Toward this purpose, I've incorporated quotes from Chekhov's plays into the dialogue (again, from my own translations).

For those of you who are interested to learn more about the lives of these two remarkable people, I recommend the following biographies: of Olga, Harvey Pitcher's *Chekhov's Leading Lady;* of Anton, among the many fine ones, Henri Troyat's lyrical *Chekhov* is my favorite, Ernest Simmon's *Chekhov* and Donald Rayfield's *Anton Chekhov* are scholarly and informative, and V. S. Pritchett's *A Spirit Set Free* is poetic.

In these biographies, you will find many and varied interpretations of their relationship. Some biographers suggest that the marriage never would have lasted, had they actually lived together. Chekhov himself wrote to his publisher, Suvorin: "Give me a wife, who, like the moon, does not appear in my sky every night." And in another letter: "Alas, I am incapable of such a complex, tangled business as marriage. And the role of husband scares me — it's stern, like a military commander's." Other biographers suggest that the lady, too, "doth protest too much" — and that, although she reproached herself constantly over her absence from her invalid husband's bedside, Olga would not have enjoyed a domestic marital routine, either. With her mercurial personality and unpredictable, artistic temperament, she was, above all, an actress, and committed to her work.

In the final analysis, the letters provide the richest material for a play. They speak for themselves. And still, they hold their own mysteries and ambiguities. Reading hers, one has the sense that she writes for posterity. Reading his, one has the sense that he hides, deflects, obscures his feelings — in a truly "Chekhovian" fashion, of course. ("Answer me truthfully, Anton: no jokes!" she often wrote him). For after all, does anyone really know about the true inner workings of a marriage? Anybody's marriage, no less theirs. Ultimately, the secrets of Anton and Olga's marriage are known to no one. The truth is left to our imaginations, and the needs and projections of our own hearts.

I dedicate this play to Olympia and Louis, to Marisa and Eric, and to all of us who love the plays of Anton Chekhov, and who love a love story. I hope that I've done theirs justice.

Carol Rocamora
December, 1999

*Note: I have translated the excerpts of their letters that appear in the dialogue of this play directly from the following original sources: *Polnoe Sobranie Sochineniy (The Complete Collected Works of Anton Chekhov)* for his letters to her; and *Perepiska A. P. Chekhova i Olgi Leonardovni Knipper (The Correspondence of A. P. Chekhov and Olga Leonardovna Knipper)* and *Olga Leonardovna Knippera-Chekhova: Vospominania i Stati. Perepiska s A.P. Chekhovim. (Reminiscences and Essays of Olga Leonardovna Knipper-Chekhova. Correspondence with A.P. Chekhov),* for her memoirs and her letters to him. (See bibliography on page 49).

" I take your hand in mine . . . "

Cast of Characters

The characters in the play are a man and a woman, telling the story of the relationship between Anton Chekhov and Olga Knipper. When reading the narrative, they are actor and actress. As they segue into the letters and spontaneous dialogue, they become the characters of Anton Chekhov and Olga Knipper.

Setting

The stage is bare. The action of the play can be staged simply, as a reading — two desks, chairs, and small lamps — or two armchairs, or two high-backed stools with music stands and clip lights. A table with a decanter of water and two glasses, perhaps some books and photographs (of Chekhov, Knipper, Chekhov's family, the Moscow Art Theatre, etc.), stands to the side.

The play is performed without an interval. There is the suggestion of scenes and an epilogue, punctuated by brief musical interludes (optional — to be used at the director's discretion). The music can consist of a live guitar playing Russian "romances" (popular nineteenth-century Russian songs of the day — Chekhov's favorites, many of which can be found in his plays), or it can be taped. It should always be delicate and unobtrusive.

As the actors enter, lights rise gradually and guitar music plays softly. The actors are seated. They illuminate the lights on their desks/music stands. The music fades.

SHE: "I take your hand in mine . . ." *(Opens script.)*

HE: "I take your hand in mine . . ." *(Opens script.)*

SHE: That's how he signed them . . . his letters to her . . . his letters to Olga . . . .

HE: Four hundred letters he wrote to her . . .

SHE: Four hundred and twelve, to be exact . . . She wrote almost as many . . .

HE: And they knew each other only six short years . . .

SHE: That's all? . . .

HE: That's all . . .

SHE: First as friends . . . .

HE: Friends? I suppose you could call it that . . .

SHE: Then as lovers . . . Then as husband and wife . . .

HE: A lifetime of love in six short years . . .

SHE: He was a writer . . .

HE: She was an actress . . .

SHE: And they met — how did they meet?

HE: I forget! . . .

SHE: You forget?! . . . At a reading . . . a reading! . . .

HE: Ah! . . . . *the* reading . . .

SHE: Of *The Seagull!* April, 1898. Remember? "My darling, you are the last page of my life!" My favorite line — how I loved to say it . . .

HE: I loved to hear her say it . . . I wrote those lines . . . Though not for her, actually . . . I didn't know her when I wrote them . . . And yet, when she read them, oh when she read them . . . I thrill to remember it . . . She was twenty-nine years old . . .

SHE: He was thirty-eight . . . and so famous . . . so famous . . . I'll never forget it . . . Our very first season . . . A fledgling new company . . . Nemirovich insisted . . . "We've got to have *The Seagull,*" he said . . . "I want Chekhov . . ."

HE: I told them they were crazy . . . "It's a terrible play," I said . . . "They hated it in Petersburg . . . The reviewers killed it . . ."

SHE: Stanislavsky said: "I must direct it!"

HE: The Moscow Art Theatre! . . . Nice name . . .

SHE: We all gathered, the company that is, and read through the script for him . . . We were trembling when he arrived . . .

HE: I remember: All I could hear was her voice . . .

SHE: He seemed so detached . . .

HE: "Who is that actress?" I asked lightly . . . "Olga Knipper," they said, "One of Nemirovich's pupils!"

SHE: He loved to joke . . . We asked him: "What does it mean, the play? Tell us, Anton Pavlovich, tell us, please!" Like children, we were . . .

HE: "What does it mean? Simple! It's all there in the stage directions!" . . .

SHE: How we laughed! He loved to make us laugh . . .

HE: I passed around some chocolates . . .

SHE: He talked about the weather . . . Our eyes met for a moment . . . I think he was still laughing . . .

HE: I was squinting, actually . . . Those pince-nez are hard to balance on one's nose, you know . . .

SHE: We didn't know what to say . . . He looked at us, smiling, then suddenly he was serious . . .

HE: They rehearsed all evening in that cold, unfinished theater . . . without a floor, with candle-ends in bottles instead of lamps, bundled in their overcoats — what a sight they were! . . .

SHE: What joy to think that somewhere out there in the dark, empty stalls was the soul we so adored, listening to us . . .

HE: I went back to Yalta, to my prison by the sea . . . *(Coughs.)*

SHE: Imagine — he missed the opening! December in Moscow was too cruel for him. But he came back in the spring . . . We performed it one afternoon, especially for him . . .

HE: She was . . . electrifying! . . .

SHE: "My joy, my pride, my ecstacy . . . Leave me, even for one hour, and I won't survive, I'll go mad, my glorious, marvelous man, my master! . . ."

HE: Charismatic! . . .

SHE: ". . . You're mine . . . This forehead is mine, and these eyes are mine, and this wonderful silky hair is mine, too . . . You're all mine! You're so talented, so brilliant, the best of living writers, you're the one hope of Russia! You'll go with me? Yes? You won't desert me?"

HE: ". . . I have no will of my own . . ."

SHE: Those were the lines! . . .

HE: That was it for me! . . .

SHE: I remember that sunny Easter day, the joyful ringing of the bells, the air filled with expectation . . . And suddenly, without warning —

HE: I called on her family. She was German, you know . . .

SHE: Chekhov, who never called on anyone. What a happy sunny day! I went with him to an exhibition — his artist friend Levitan's.

HE: In May she came to Melikhovo, to my "estate," south of Moscow . . .

SHE: I loved his mother . . . a gentle Russian woman, so proud . . .

HE: She didn't love my sister, that's for certain —

SHE: I *loved* his sister, Masha . . .

HE: — though, of course, she said she did, and my brothers . . . I showed her my domain: a pond with carp, my garden —

SHE: He loved his garden, he loved all earthly offerings . . . I found it so enchanting: the house, the little dacha—

HE: — where I'd written *The Seagull*, the winding paths, the flowering fruit trees, the calves, the ducks —

SHE: — and the village school mistress, running along the road with her pupils . . .

HE: Three glorious days she visited us . . .

SHE: Three days filled with joy, and sunlight, and promise of the future . . . Then I went to the Caucasus to see my family, and our correspondence began . . .

HE: "What's happening? Where are you?"

SHE: His first letter to me, from Melikhovo. June 16, 1899 . . .

HE: "Your writer has been forgotten, how cruel, how callous. I'm back in Melikhovo now, on my 'estate.' No news from here. No flies, either. Nothing. Even the calves aren't biting. Won't be going to Yalta before early July . . . I take your hand in mine, that is, if you'll allow me . . ."

SHE: That first letter . . . the first of so many . . .

HE: "I take your hand in mine, dear actress . . ."

(Music.)

SHE: At the time, he was building his house in Yalta. His doctors were banishing him to the south, and he had to leave his beloved Melikhovo . . . The consumption was progressing . . .

HE: She was rehearsing in Moscow . . . I journeyed south to Yalta on the train . . .

SHE: "You've only been gone four days and already I need to write you. I know it's too soon, but I can't help myself! Saturday evening, my favorite, the sound of the church bells is so peaceful . . ."

HE: You sentimental German, you . . .

SHE: "I was so sad at the station when you left, I felt like crying all the way home . . . Your sister was here yesterday. How nice of her!"

HE: Checking up on you . . .

SHE: "How was the journey?"

HE: "Fine. Fine. My companions let me take the lower berth. I ate everything in the basket. No boiling water on the train for tea, though. Arrived at my house in Yalta last evening. It's so quiet here. I sat indoors, thinking of you . . . My dear dear actress, if only you knew what pleasure your letters give me. I bow low before you, very low, so low, in fact, that my brow touches the bottom of a well eight fathoms deep."

SHE: "Thanks for the photographs and the sweets. And for your letters, too. I was so distraught, I thought you didn't want to write to me . . . This morning we rehearsed *Uncle Vanya*. Tonight I play Arkadina in *The Seagull*. Stanislavsky can't come to *Vanya* rehearsals — he's directing *Ivan the Terrible*. How is he going to play Astrov if he's not at rehearsals?!

HE: Good luck . . . He's not a bad director, but he's a terrible actor!

SHE: "Why don't you write more often? Don't you feel the need?"

HE: "Nothing to write about. It's so lonely and dull here. I feel I've been living in Yalta a million years. Today I caught two mice . . . I press your hand in mine, busy actress, don't forget me . . ."

SHE: "October 26, 1899: Opening night of *Uncle Vanya!* I was so excited! Was I all right in Act IV? —*(Plays.)* 'You're an unusual man . . . unique. We'll never see each other again, so why hide it! I was attracted to you in a way . . .' "

HE: *(Plays.)* " 'Go, then. *Finita la commedia.*' "

SHE: *(Plays.)* " 'I'm keeping this pencil as a remembrance . . .' "

HE: Brava, dear actress! Sounds wonderful to me!

SHE: "How they loved it! I telegrammed right after the performance!"

HE: "I know, they rang me. I ran to the phone in the dark, barefoot — God, the floor was cold! — then hardly had I gotten back into bed, when it rang once again! The only time in my life when my own fame kept me awake!"

SHE: "I was terrible. Abominable. The play was a success, the audience raved, and what do I do? — I act appallingly. Had to take valerian drops to calm myself. 'You have no idea how it feels to know you're acting badly!' You wrote that yourself! Remember?"

HE: "You're over-reacting, really you are. A few bad performances are no reason to feel low. Art, especially the theater, is a world you cannot enter without stumbling over the threshold. There are many days of failure ahead, whole seasons, even, things will go badly, you will have huge heartbreak, but you must prepare for it, expect it and follow your path."

SHE: "Come see me! I need you!"

HE: "Be calm, dear actress! Success has spoiled you . . . Ordinary every-day life just isn't good enough . . ."

SHE: "How I suffer from my work! One day I'm up, the next day I'm down . . . For the love of God, write!"

HE: "I write you so often that it's hurting my pride. I must treat my little actress more severely and not write to her. Be well, my angel. I kiss your little hand. I envy the coat you wear every day."

SHE: "I feel so low. It's awful . . ."

HE: "But why? You're alive, you're working, you have hopes, what more could you want? Look at me. I'm uprooted from my native soil. I don't drink, though I love to, I like noise and there's none here, I'm like a transplanted tree . . . Do I wither away and die? No. I rage with jealousy. I envy the rat that lives under your theater's floor."

SHE: "New Year's Eve! Tonight we played *Uncle Vanya!*"

HE: 1900. Imagine — the Centennial! "Happy New Year, my remarkable actress . . ."

SHE: "There was thunderous applause! It was thrilling! We're taking it to Petersburg!"

HE: "How I wish I could see it! It's cold here, cold and quiet as the grave. Write to me, please, I'm so bored. I feel as if I'm in prison. Come to Yalta in the spring! To celebrate the Centennial! Why don't you?!"

SHE: "We're coming! In April! The whole company's coming! We'll bring the set of *Uncle Vanya!* We'll perform it especially for you!"

HE: "Dear actress: It's March, at last! Lilies, irises, hyacinths — all are in bloom. The willow is blossoming; the grass round the bench is lush and luxuriant. The almond tree flowers. All nature is expecting you. I've put benches everywhere in preparation for your arrival, wooden ones, which I've painted green myself. I'm planting palms."

SHE: "How wonderful! We'll be in Yalta at Easter time. That means we'll see each other so soon!"

HE: "We've taken off our galoshes, and go out only in hats now. I've haven't heard a note of music since autumn. You will bring the music . . ."

SHE: We came in April . . . It was like a festival . . . We arrived in Yalta, and were strewn with flowers. We performed *Uncle Vanya* for him. Rachmaninoff was there, and Gorky . . . Bunin and Kuprin . . . Tolstoy, too . . . It was glorious . . .

HE: Every moment of it I treasured . . . Lunches, dinners, parties till all hours . . . I entertained them day and night . . .

SHE: We swarmed all over his little house, sat in his study, wandered in his almond orchard . . .

HE: A whirlwind of life and laughter and hope . . .

SHE: We left the swing and bench from *Vanya* in his garden . . .

HE: "Must you leave so soon?"

SHE: "We must . . . the Petersburg spring tour . . . you know . . ."

HE: I came to Moscow soon thereafter . . . It was so empty in Yalta after they'd gone . . . I couldn't bear it . . .

SHE: But he was not feeling well, so back he went . . . In June, I journeyed by train to Yalta, to the wonderful, luxuriant south . . . The gentle sun, the scent-laden air . . . "We're travelling in a carriage with two large Armenian ladies . . . I'm counting the miles!"

HE: She arrived in early July . . . The azaleas were in bloom . . .

SHE: In July, we became lovers . . .

(Music.)

SHE: August 6, 1900. "Good morning, my darling! I'm sitting on the train, drinking very bad coffee, trying to write you. The carriage sways dangerously. I'm looking out the window now, stretches of endless space as we move ever northward — why northward? — you are in the south! Feel my burning kisses. A lady sitting opposite me, an admirer of our theater, says she's seen *The Seagull* four times. She didn't suspect she was talking to Arkadina. I didn't enlighten her. Addio, Antonioni. Love me, write to me."

HE: "My glorious actress: I'm here in Yalta, my prison. A cruel wind is blowing, the boats aren't running, the sea is swelling, people are drowning — in a word, it's been awful since you've gone. Without you, I shall hang myself. Giant kisses, 400 of them. Be well, my little doggie . . ."

SHE: Call me Olga. Call me by my name.

HE: I will, golubchik . . . I will, my little German . . .

SHE: "It's terrible without you, I want to hold you, caress you, I feel as if I've been cast overboard. Are you lonely? Are you working? Do you eat well? Do you love me? Do you quarrel with your mother? Answer every question I ask you. I hold your dear head and kiss you good night."

HE: "My treasure: It's September. Yalta is empty. The trees are withering, the stream is drying up, even the crane is bored. I don't know when I'm coming to Moscow, because, believe it or not, I'm writing a play — well, not exactly a play, a sort of hodgepodge. There are so many characters I get confused. I don't know . . ."

SHE: A play?!

HE: "Yes, a play. It's in my head, it's simply begging to be written down, but as soon as I pick up a pen, some frightful-looking face peers through the door . . ."

SHE: A new play . . . by Chekhov!

HE: "These constant guests are an infernal nuisance. Yesterday they were here from morning till night. My head is in a muddle, my mood is mercurial, I get angry and have to start all over every day. You can't imagine the menagerie! The headmistress of the local girls' school just arrived with two of her companions. They've installed themselves in my study and now they're drinking tea. I'll never get rid of them!"

SHE: "Is there a part for me?!"

HE: "Ah, what a part, what a part I have for you! Give me ten rubles and you can have it, or else I'll give it to another actress!"

SHE: "Oh hurry, finish it!"

HE: "I can't. There's a very large lady in grey, wandering in my garden. I'm watching her from the window as I hide in the study. God, what a dress! With a green belt! Who *is* she? I can't bear all these interruptions!! A play needs to be written in one sitting!"

SHE: "My darling, get rid of all those people! Throw them out! . . . *The Three Sisters?* I like the title. Which one am I?"

HE: "I don't feel like working on the play anymore, it all seems so vulgar to me! There are so many characters, crowds of them, and I'm afraid it will be too confusing. Be patient, my angel. I'll reward you for it. I'll love you wildly, like an Arab, all night long . . ."

SHE: "Like an Arab?! Hurry to Moscow, my darling!"

HE: "Can't come yet. One of the sisters has developed a limp, she's shaky, I can't do anything with her. And anyway, I'm afraid to come to Moscow. My hair is falling out, it's awful. I hide at home."

SHE: "Don't worry about your hair. I've got an excellent remedy for baldness: It's my Uncle Sasha's."

HE: "A recipe for baldness? How charming! I'll put it in the play some-where, my dove . . . I can't rush it, darling. The play needs to sit awhile, or as the cooks say, lie out on the counter, like a freshly baked pie, and breathe . . ."

SHE: "You're always joking! Must you? Enough! Finish the play!"

HE: "October 14: The play is finished. I'm coming!"

SHE: "Come as fast as you can!"

HE: "I'll swim!"

SHE: He came in November . . . We were discreet . . . He stayed at the Hotel Dresden, but we were together as much as we could be . . . His mother and Masha, after all . . .

HE: The Art Theatre read *The Three Sisters* aloud on November 17 . . . There was a stunned silence . . .

SHE: He wandered among us, laughing and joking . . . But we couldn't disguise it . . . We were bewildered . . .

HE: They didn't understand my play . . . Revisions on Act I, then away . . . Away from it all . . . *(Coughs.)*

SHE: You're going?

HE: I must . . . It's December . . . The winter's here . . .

SHE: But what about the rest of the revisions? Don't leave yet —

HE: I'll send them from Nice!

SHE: Nice . . . "My dearest darling: Yesterday at the station, as your train pulled away, I ran after it and burst into torrents of tears. Our separation, the reality of it . . . I stood at the end of the platform so the others couldn't see me. Take care changing trains, and for God's sake stay warm . . . Why do you always have to go?"

HE: "I'm in Vienna, my Knipperschitz. The shops are all shut, it's German Christmas! So here I am, alone in my room, looking at the two beds, feeling foolish. I'll rush to the post office when I get to Nice. Huge kisses."

SHE: Nice . . . The sun, the sea . . . Three months apart . . .

HE: "*Salue, ma belle:* Nice, at last. The *Pension Russe.* Rooms full of Russians. I'll go down to the sea, and read the papers in the sunshine. Then back to the hotel to start the rewrites. 10,000 kisses. *Ton Antoine.*"

SHE: "Minus twenty-seven degrees. Moscow is frozen. I walk the streets and everything hurts — my eyes, my cheeks, my lips. I cry, I have no energy. A raging temperature and a painful cough —"

HE: "I have a remedy for your flu, my angel. A huge hug, a kiss, and yet another hug. Happy New Year, my sweet. *Felicité, bonheur, argent, gloire.* Imagine, 1901 already. It's going so fast! . . ."

SHE: "Rehearsing *Sisters* by day, playing *Vanya* by night. The doctor has given me quinine, I drink tea with rum. Stanislavsky and Nemirovich are crazed, waiting for the Act III and IV revisions! Where are they?!"

HE: "Cheer up, golubchik! I'm sending them tomorrow."

SHE: "We have the revisions! Naphthaline? How delightful! Uncle Sasha's remedy for baldness! He'll be so pleased! . . . Must Masha wear black in *every* act, my darling?"

HE: Yes, she must. But don't look despondent, not in one single scene!

Angry, yes; despondent, no. People who are sad inside simply whistle, they're lost in thought. You become pensive while others talk. Understand? And send me news of rehearsals! I don't trust Stanislavsky with four women's roles! Write to me, my Jewess."

SHE: "My flu is still raging. We worked on Act IV today. You've given me so many new lines, my darling. 'When you snatch at happiness in bits and pieces, and then you lose it, as I have, little by little you grow coarse, and bitter. Deep inside me, a rage is burning . . .' My God, how do I play that? And what about: 'In a cove by the sea, a green oak stands, a golden chain wound round, a golden chain wound round . . .?'"

HE: Keep it light and real . . . Remember, you're easily amused and easily angered . . . Simple and real . . .

SHE: "If only you could see the set! It's charming. A lovely pathway, lined with birch trees, a house with a terrace where the officers gather . . . Does it matter if I make a tiny cut in my final speech? Nemirovich says it sounds too much like Sonya's in *Uncle Vanya*. Masha is a marvel. If I ruin her, I'll leave acting forever!"

HE: You won't . . . I wrote her for you . . .

SHE: "Darling! This is urgent! Stanislavksy has asked me to write to you about the end of Act IV. Must we carry Tusenbach's body across the stage? It would mean that a crowd scene would break up the trio of sisters, and also, the set would wobble, since it's not very deep. For God's sake, answer immediately! We sisters can't just sit there while a body is carted through the garden, can we?!"

HE: I told you Stanislavsky doesn't understand my work . . .

SHE: "A crisis in Act III! The song which Vershinin and Masha hum to one another — how should we do it? Nemirovich thinks we should sound it out like bugle calls: 'Tram tam tam!' What a horrible idea! And we open in only ten days! Help me, Toto, I'm lost without you!"

HE: "If Stanislavsky ruins Act III, the whole play is lost, and so is my reputation! Sound effects? My God, what is he doing?! There's only the noise from the fire, distant and faint, while on stage it is still! And my dearest, Masha's speech isn't a confession — it's just a frank conversation. Play it with some tension, but don't be desperate, don't raise your voice, smile from time to time, and above all, feel the exhaustion of the night."

SHE: " 'I have something to confess, darling sisters . . . My soul is in anguish . . .' "

HE: That's it . . .

SHE: " 'I shall confess it to you and you alone, and never again to anyone, anywhere . . . And I shall tell it to you now. It's my secret, but you should know everything . . . I cannot keep silent . . .' "

HE: Gently . . . Gently . . . And stay on the sofa, be still . . . Let Irina come to you . . .

SHE: " 'I love, love, love this man . . . You've only just seen him. There, now you know. I love Vershinin . . .' "

HE: That's it . . . A little more urgency . . .

SHE: " 'What can I do? At first, I thought him strange, then I pitied him, then I fell in love with him . . . with his voice, his words, his misfortunes, his two little girls. I love him — that is my fate. That is my lot in life, you see. And he loves me. It's all so awful. Isn't it?' "

HE: Smile, my angel . . .

SHE: " 'Isn't it?! Oh, my sisters . . . Somehow we shall live through life, whatever it has in store for us . . . My darlings, my sisters . . . There, I've confessed to you, and now I shall be silent . . . Like Gogol's madman . . . Silence . . . Silence . . . Tram-tam-tam . . .'"

HE: " 'Tam-tam . . .'"

SHE: " 'Tra-ra-ra . . .'"

HE: " 'Tra-ta-ta'! That one I leave to you. You are my interpreter!"

SHE: January 31: Moscow. Telegram: *"Les Trois Soeurs: Un Grand Succes. Je t'embrace . . ."* Anton, where are you? I thought you were in Algiers? . . .

HE: "No, my pigeon . . . Florence . . . People who haven't been to Italy haven't lived . . . Then on to Naples, then Corfu, then Constantinople, if there isn't the plague . . . Your telegram arrived today after a whole week. I thought the play had flopped —"

SHE: *"The Three Sisters* is the talk of Moscow! They write: 'Miss Knipper shines in a superb ensemble!' Aren't you proud?! I'm so sad you can't see me as Masha. I'd play her for you with such joy!"

HE: More details, I beg of you . . . Send them to Rome . . .

SHE: "Where are you, my Anton? I can't keep track! Last night there was a standing ovation. We're going to Petersburg next week. Sold out already. We open with *Vanya.* Tonight we play *The Seagull.* Everyone's talking about Chekhov, Chekhov, Chekhov . . . When are you returning to Russia?"

HE: Soon, soon . . . "You'll come to Yalta, won't you?"

SHE: *(Pause.)* "I can't. . . I can't come to Yalta . . . Don't you see? What's the point? To hide the truth once again from your mother and sister, to see them awkward and embarrassed . . . Your mother's silence, the angry look on Masha's face . . . I can't bear it!"

HE: Nonsense!

SHE: "How much longer can we go on pretending? Come to Moscow. Marry me, and we'll live together. Shall we, dear Anton? Answer me seriously, just this once!"

HE: "I can't marry you. At our wedding, I'll look like your grandfather, not your husband. And anyway I'm giving up literature — it's not good for me, so if we marry, you'll have to give up the theater, too, and we'll live together like farmers."

SHE: "I said no jokes, Antonio, no jokes . . ."

HE: "All right then, dear actress. All right, little Knippschitz . . . Give me your word that *no one* in Moscow will know about our marriage until it has actually happened, and I'll come up from Yalta and marry you the day I arrive. For some strange reason I dread weddings: the congratulations, the embraces, the standing around with an idiotic grin on one's face . . . Not a word to anyone, promise? And afterwards, we'll swim down the Volga like two little sturgeons! Your fool in love, Antoine."

SHE: "A honeymoon on the Volga? I'm as happy as a child. I've never seen the Volga. My heart is so full of light! Oh — don't forget your passport, my darling. You can't get married without one . . ."

HE: "I'm leaving for Moscow on May 10. *(Coughs.)* Tell your actor who plays Vanya — Vishnievsky, is it? — that I don't plan to die in the very near future. He's counting on the fact that you'll soon be a widow, but tell him I'm vengeful and am writing a will in which you're forbidden to remarry. I hug you, traitress, a hundred times."

SHE: He came, as planned . . . All our friends and relatives were invited to dinner on May 25 . . . a lovely little restaurant in Moscow . . . They waited and waited for the bridal couple . . .

HE: . . . who never appeared . . .

SHE: Then finally the news arrived at the restaurant that —

HE: Surprise surprise!!!!

SHE: *(Laughs.)* They'd already been married on the other side of town, and had set out on their honeymoon . . .

HE: *(Laughs.)* Can you imagine their faces?!

SHE: He did forget his passport, by the way . . . But the ceremony proceeded, somehow . . . They sailed down the Volga, to a sanatorium at Aksyonovo, where he could rest . . . What a lovely spot: a beautiful oak forest, primitive, dark, mysterious . . .

HE: The long shadows on the steppe in the evening, the shining herds of horses, the flora, the fauna . . .

SHE: We fished every day on the Dyoma River . . .

HE: I love to fish . . .

SHE: He was so happy . . .

HE: " 'If I lived on an estate like that, by a lake, I wonder if I'd ever have been a writer. I'd give up this obsession, and do nothing but fish . . . I'd catch ruff, or perch — what bliss!' "

SHE: What bliss . . .

(Music.)

HE: "August 23, 1901. My wondrous wife: Back again in Yalta, my prison, my hot Siberia. How is Moscow? Your armchair is lonely. Your room is silent. I didn't brush my clothes today. My boots haven't been polished, either — your absence is keenly felt. Write to me every day, or else you'll be beaten. I'm a very stern husband, remember that . . ."

SHE: "My darling husband: Back again in Moscow. How I dreaded returning! The carriage ride was awful; I wept the whole way. As soon as I arrived, I went straight to the theater. Nemirovich barraged me with questions: Would I give up the theater? Would you come for the winter? I'm pining here without you. What are you thinking, what are you dreaming? Did you get my letters? Do they tidy your room? Answer every question! I send you hot, hot kisses . . ."

HE: "Don't worry, darling, Masha's coming, she'll see to everything!"

SHE: *Masha?!* . . . "*I* should be there taking care of you . . ."

HE: "Yesterday, I washed my hair in alcohol, just as you told me to, I change my shirt every day, too . . . I embrace you, dearest doggie, I kiss both your little paws . . ."

SHE: "It's October already. Today the sun is warm, there's a smell of autumn leaves . . . I've gotten a kitten for our new apartment! If you don't like it, it can stay in the kitchen. It's sweet, gentle and plump; it sneezes, and rubs its eyes with its paws . . ."

HE: "Keep a crocodile if you want, I don't care . . . As long as I have you . . . Masha and mother are still here —"

SHE: "How wildly jealous I am! I'm so ashamed — I have such savage thoughts. I want to take you away, away from them! Anton, help me!"

HE: "A little half-German! That's what you need! I want you to have one, to fill your life!"

SHE: "Yes, yes, a little half-German! Grisha, we'll call him! I curse myself for not giving up the theater! Come to Moscow, darling!"

HE: "I can't come now, you know that, not till spring. Yesterday I went to see Tolstoy. He's old now, but still, he's fine company. The Countess took a photograph of us. I'll send it.

SHE: "I framed it, I kiss it every day. Anton, I'm so lonely. I don't make your bed — I pretend you're here, and my thoughts run so wildly out of control . . ."

HE: "Don't worry, krinolinchik, winter will pass quickly, and we'll be together all spring."

SHE: "But how will I get through the winter? I want to be with you. I want to know what's in every corner of your mind. Am I being too bold, or is entry forbidden? Anton, I despair. I want a life with you. I want our mornings together, with you sitting on the bed, after washing, without your vest, with your back to me. You see what thoughts I have, Anton, and others I won't mention . . ."

HE: "Can't you come to Yalta for Christmas, Knippusha? Nemirovich is a tyrant; you'll sit around doing nothing for the holidays."

SHE: "I'll talk to him and find out the Christmas schedule. They're working me to death. I get home at four in the morning, and then we rehearse every day. I'm writing to you from my dressing room. Makeup, powder, dust everywhere. I'm in my wig with curlers, all greasy and exhausted. Anton, what's happening? I'm in such confusion. Can't you come to Moscow?"

HE: "Haven't been well for the past few days. Loneliness is affecting my stomach. And I'm coughing a lot. Forty-one — and already I'm an old man. Won't they let you come see your lonely old monk?"

SHE: "Rehearsed all day and played all night. The 500th performance of the Moscow Art Theatre! I'm quite drunk, Anton! Forgive your dissolute wife! After the show, we gathered in Nemirovich's office and celebrated. Pies, caviar, salmon, fruit, wine, champagne — God, how Vishnievsky drank! We laughed and laughed! We toasted you, of course, my darling!"

HE: "My intemperate wife: How I envy you, my sweetheart. Your spirit, your health, the fact that you drink without spitting blood —"

SHE: "Bad news, darling: I'm performing every evening over the holidays. Can you imagine? I'm sick of it! I'll wither and die without love and affection. I have such needs!"

HE: "How was the opening of *In Dreams*, dear Knippusha? I waited all day for a telegram. It was a success and you've forgotten me . . ."

SHE: "It was! A *huge* success! Forgive me for not writing — I haven't slept in nights. Oh Anton, you should see my costume! It's brilliant crimson. And the train is all sequined. They say the *decolleté* is gorgeous. You wouldn't recognize me! I play the role fast, you know, *à la française*. The papers say I'm too bold. Stanislavsky likes it, though. And Vishnievsky says I'm divine . . . After the opening, we all went to a restaurant, and stayed up till the papers came at seven in the morning. Vishnievsky was drunk, he talked all night; I invited him back . . . with a few others, of course. We drank morning coffee and laughed and laughed. I finally got to bed at eleven, then up at three for lunch and back to the theater. What do you think of this crazy life?"

HE: "At a restaurant till morning again? Listen, Knipperschitz, you mustn't ruin your health . . . As for me, I'm still running a fever . . . ."

SHE: "How it pains me that I can't be with you, to nurse you, change your compresses, feed you. I'm such a bad wife. You're sorry you married me, say it, go on —"

HE: "Don't worry, darling, I'll get better . . ."

SHE: "The holidays . . . What a foul mood I'm in . . . Stanislavsky spent hours consoling me. He says I must work harder and that it's good that we're apart . . ."

HE: "Merry Christmas, my angel. There's only one thing missing in my life . . . my wife . . ."

SHE: "Wait till spring, my darling . . . I shall take you abroad, care for you and bore you to death. We'll have our little Grisha. I'll give up the theater, I promise —"

HE: "Listen to me, my little goose: Never, as long as I'm your husband, will I ever take you away from the theater. So don't talk nonsense. It's New Year's Eve. I'm going to bed at nine. You're not here, so I don't have to see the New Year in. 1902, imagine. The weather's getting worse. If it's snowing here, I may as well be in Moscow . . . 'To Moscow! To Moscow!' . . ."

SHE: "My dearest, I'm so busy I don't see the light of day. I've already played five performances straight. Starting tomorrow, I shall play seven more. And we're out all night after. I'm so keyed up, I can't go to sleep. Happy New Year, my poet . ."

HE: "My darling Knipperschitz, what's going on? . . . You're being a good little wife . . . aren't you?"

SHE: "The seventh performance in a row; tonight, *Uncle Vanya*. If only you'd been here! At the end, they presented the theater with your portrait, a huge one, framed in gold — very tasteful, I assure you — there was thunderous applause, and shouts of 'author! author!' After the show, we had a splendid meal and drank champagne. Home at nine this morning, exhausted. I'll sleep now. Oh, I sent you sweets for your birthday, my love — did you receive them?"

HE: "No sweets yet. It's sunny and quiet in Yalta. Only the timid chirping of the birds, who will fly to Moscow soon. How I envy those birds . . . Listen, Knippusha, you *are* being a good wife, aren't you?"

SHE: "Tired today, bone tired. Feeling more and more closed in. And so alone, though there are people around me all the time. You're unhappy with me, aren't you? You write to me less and less."

HE: "I've so little to say, my love. And you're so busy . . . Yes, the sweets arrived. They were a trifle stale. Never mind . . . Forty-two yesterday . . . I feel seventy-two. Stay home, my darling, get some rest. I kiss your sweet face, I stroke your lovely little back. . ."

SHE: "Another performance again tonight . . . The ninth in a row . . ."

HE: "Haven't heard from you in days. Out late again, my dissolute darling? Promise to think of your husband when you come in, before you go to bed . . ."

(Pause.)

Olga? . . . Is something the matter? . . .

SHE: "Darling, I've finally summoned up the courage to write to you. I don't know how to tell you this . . . Call me all the names you like . . . I have debts, many debts, huge ones, which I must pay. When I tell you, you'll be horrified. I owe 7000 rubles —"

HE: 7000!!! . . . For what? . . . You mean *700,* don't you? . . .

SHE: "No, 7000. Terrible, isn't it? I want to pay it off in installments, but it's not possible. You've just had a royalty of 8000 from the theater.

If you decide to help me, I'll be so grateful. I'll pay it off, I promise. If only you knew how hard it is to write this. I'm so ashamed. Don't tell your mother or Masha — God, no . . ."

HE: Yes . . . Of course . . . Only . . . let us not speak of it again . . .

SHE: "Days pass, and not a line from you. Tonight is a gala — the 100th performance of *The Three Sisters*. And a huge party afterwards, huge. Maybe I'll write the day after tomorrow. I'm so tired. Don't fall out of love with me, my darling . . ."

HE: Don't forget me, my wife . . .

(Pause.)

SHE: *(Abruptly.)* "Arriving in Yalta in a week. Plan to stay two days. Wire to confirm."

HE: What? "You're coming to Yalta for two days? Why now? Thank Nemirovich for his act of charity, but *two* days? If we've held out this long, we can hold out till Lent. What will two days achieve? You'll be exhausted from the journey, I might be ill — who knows? We'll only have time for good-byes —"

SHE: "I leave Moscow on Friday . . . I count the moments till we are together. The only thing that upsets me is that *Uncle Vanya*'s on, and Stanislavsky's wife will play Yelena in my absence! I'm wild with jealousy . . ."

HE: "If there's talk of a storm at sea, then don't take the boat: Go straight to the coach station and take a covered barouche, or better yet, a carriage. I'm counting the days . . ."

SHE: "Arriving tomorrow morning . . ."

HE: She came, and stayed five days, not two . . . Why had she come? . . .

(Music.)

SHE: "My dearest darling, my only husband, I've left you yet again . . . I'm at the station, it's dark and dreary, I can't get tea or anything hot to eat. After we passed through Lombat, it began to snow; there was a blizzard in Alush, and thereafter, severe frost. I'm writing in the ladies' room with my face all wrapped up. Why, oh why didn't I kiss you once again on the terrace? I thought about it the whole journey long . . ."

HE: "My dearest wife: I'm worried sick about the weather. Your visit felt so rushed. There was hardly any time. Hurry back. I can't live without my wife . . ."

SHE: "I'm travelling second class back to Moscow, there weren't any seats in first. A lady from Yalta sat opposite me. She asked me if I liked Chekhov, the writer. Of course I didn't tell her who I was. Before the train left, I felt quite strange. Pain in my stomach, nausea, palpitations, I almost passed out. I've never felt like this before. I was so afraid, I thought I wouldn't be able to travel —"

HE: Nausea? . . .

SHE: " — and when I told my companion of my symptoms, she said I might be in an 'interesting' condition . . . It occured to me, too. I was so frightened, I dashed to the ladies room and collapsed. My stomach was upset. We'll see . . ."

HE: Wait . . . that's not possible . . . We were only just together . . .

SHE: "Back in Moscow . . . No letters from you, none at all . . . It's a dull grey day, thawing, slushy, I'm nauseous, and in a vile mood. Stayed in bed all day . . . Anton, I don't want to appear on the stage. I don't want to act any more. What does it mean? Endless performances of *Sisters:* 'We must live . . . We must live . . .' How boring . . . Sometimes I hate the theater, other times I love it to distraction . . .

It has given me joy and sorrow . . . It has given me you . . . Why didn't we meet as different people?"

HE: "My angel, your reviews in *The Three Sisters* were raves! The 'Russian Sarah Bernhardt'! Are you planning to get rid of me? Or will you engage me to count your box office! Give up the stage? You? Never! As long as we have a little Grisha one day . . ."

SHE: "So tired. After rehearsal, I came home, lay down, then went to the hairdressers. Later, Vishnievsky arrived, and we went to Kontan's restaurant with all the others. Came home after 4 A.M., slept till noon . . ."

HE: "No letter from you . . . Today I went to the dentist's . . ."

SHE: "Tomorrow is the opening of Gorky's new play, but I feel nothing, neither joy nor excitement. Yesterday I felt ill. Something in my stomach. Today I feel weak . . ."

HE: "I'm still having fillings, but it will be over soon. Miss you. . ."

(Pause.)

HE: "Doggie, I haven't heard from you in days . . . days . . ."

(Pause.)

Olga?

SHE: "I haven't written in a while, darling Anton . . . Something extra-ordinary has happened . . . Apparently I *did* leave Yalta in the hope of giving you a little Grisha, but didn't know it. I kept feeling ill and thinking it was food poisoning . . . They sent for the doctor. It was then I began to realize what the matter was . . . How I wept . . ."

HE: *(Unhearing.)* "Still no letters from you, but I suppose you're deep in rehearsals. I am going to see Tolstoy today. The weather is splendid. How was the opening of Gorky's new play?"

SHE: "I'm heartbroken there is to be no Grisha . . . Stanislavsky was here all day, pacing up and down the corridor . . . In the evening they took me to the clinic, and at midnight gave me chloroform . . ."

HE: *(Unhearing.)* "Again no letter from you today . . ."

SHE: "Dr. Ott did the operation so there's no need for you to worry. They want me flat on my back for four days, so I won't be acting, that's for certain. Don't know when they'll let me out. I've been crying a lot, but on the whole, I'm being very brave. Anton . . . are you sorry about Grisha? Your doggie is a failure . . ."

HE: *(Unhearing.)* "No word . . . Olga? . . . Is anything the matter?"

SHE: "Darling heart: My fifth day in bed. Having a very bad time. I desperately want to be near you. I need your tenderness, your caresses. I'm having acute pains on the left side of my abdomen —"

HE: *(Unhearing, overlapping.)* "It's started again, my toothache . . ."

SHE: " — the pain is unbearable. I don't know when they'll discharge me . . ."

HE: *(Unhearing.)* "Went to the dentist again . . ."

SHE: "The company has been one big, comforting family to me, surrounding me with love and warmth . . ."

HE: *(Unhearing.)* "Still no word from you . . ."

SHE: "The doctor comes every day to the clinic . . . Please tell your Mother and Masha — I couldn't face them myself —"

HE: *(Abruptly.)* — Clinic?! Olga! . . . "Have just received your letters! Wire immediately!"

SHE: "Your wife is covered in shame. The company joke is: 'Our leading actress is in disgrace. To have a child by such a man, and then lose it, smacks of sheer carelessness' . . . They say it to make me laugh, but I don't think it's funny . . ."

HE: "Wire details immediately!"

SHE: "Flat on my back and still no word from you . . . You haven't forgotten me, Anton, have you? I need your love."

HE: Why — don't — you — WIRE?!

SHE: " 'Health improving but doctor postponing discharge. Kisses wire me stop your doggie' . . . Day six. I thought I'd be leaving the clinic today, but I'm still here . . . Don't worry, there's no danger . . . I would give so much to hold you and weep. I've done a lot of weeping . . . Anton?"

HE: *(No response.)*

SHE: "Anton? . . . Less pain in my left side. I hardly eat at all. They try to tempt me with caviar. Masses of flowers still arriving. Stanislavsky visits me every day — he fusses over me as though I were his daughter. I tried to sit up in a chair today, and my legs felt as if they belonged to someone else. But that will pass . . ."

HE: "Am coming to Moscow immediately —"

SHE: No, Anton, don't . . . "I'm coming to Yalta. I've decided to leave on Thursday, and Dr. Ott advises that a midwife accompany me on the journey. He wouldn't take a kopek for the operation, but I have to pay the midwife three rubles a day. Do you approve? Dr. Ott has ordered me to be very careful for the next six months. Ask Masha to prepare my room . . ."

HE: "Expecting you any day . . ."

(Music.)

SHE: Six weeks I stayed in Yalta . . . depressed . . . despondent . . . Masha's looks, his mother's glances . . . Worst of all, his silence . . . Yalta became my prison, too . . . *(To HIM.)* Talk to me, Anton!

HE: She wanted to go back to Moscow in May, though she wasn't fully recovered . . . So we went . . . *(Coughs.)* It wasn't easy on any of us . . . She suffered acute peritonitis in June . . .

SHE: He was ill, too . . . We went to the spa in Perm. Then, in June, Stanislavsky invited us to his family estate in Lyubimovka . . .

HE: A large estate . . . wonderful gardens . . . lovely summer air . . . and an orchard . . . a cherry orchard . . .

SHE: . . . and new faces: a strange governess, an outspoken student, a surly young footman, and other local eccentrics . . . Quite a coterie. He was happy here . . . *We* were happy here . . . So many months together, uninterrupted. And away from his sister . . .

HE: A letter from Masha in Yalta, urging me to return before the onset of autumn . . .

SHE: Don't go . . .

HE: I ought to, my darling . . .

SHE: Not yet . . .

HE: It's almost September . . .

SHE: She didn't invite me . . .

HE: What do you mean? . . .

SHE: She didn't invite me to Yalta . . . in her letter . . . Masha . . . She didn't invite me . . .

(Music.)

HE: "August 17, 1902: I'm finally home, in Yalta. You're angry with me, my sweetheart, but I have no idea why. Because I left you? But I'd been with you since Easter, never leaving your side, and would never have gone had I not begun spitting blood —"

SHE: "And they blame me for it! Don't you see?! I realize your stay here did your health no good, but what do your mother and sister imagine? That I miscarried on purpose? They didn't invite me to Yalta! To my own home! Anton, what's happening to us? I'm trembling . . ."

HE: Your letter to Masha . . . When she read it, she was so quiet . . .

SHE: "I was angry . . . I don't even remember what I wrote. Oh, darling, try to understand how I feel! Dear God, if only I could make a good life for you, if only I could change, how ecstatic I would be! What can I do? How wonderful it was this summer! Five months together as man and wife! I feel such a loss . . ."

HE: "What do the doctors say? When can you return to Moscow?"

SHE: "Today. It's my last day at Lyubimovka. Autumn, a pale sun . . . When I walk through the house, my steps have such a lonely echo. All the blinds are down, only the wind moves them . . . I stood at the window, looked out on the riverbank, and thought of our Grisha. And I saw you everywhere, by the water, rod in hand, on the balcony with a newspaper. Don't laugh at me for being sentimental . . . Oh, go ahead, laugh . . . O, my orchard!"

HE: "My incomparable wife: It's cold in Yalta, colder than in Moscow. And so silent . . ."

SHE: "Back to Moscow, to an empty bed. Each night, I hold your pillow in my arms. Today we had a dress rehearsal of *The Lower Depths*. Everyone at the theater asks for you."

HE: "Went into town today for the first time since I've returned. The people on the street look like ghosts. But I don't let my spirits falter, I look to the future, to when we'll be together . . . You're getting a dog?! What kind?"

SHE: "A pedigree. His name is Schnapps. I can't wait to bring him to Yalta . . . Are you writing?"

HE: "A short story, actually . . . But not a very interesting one . . . Masha left today . . . It's the first of December. The cranes are calling. Tomorrow I'll get down to writing a play."

SHE: "A play? Wonderful! They're begging for one at the theater!"

HE: "It's going to be a comedy."

SHE: "A comedy! We're waiting for it, desperately! Stanislavsky asks about it every day. *The Cherry Orchard*, it's called? How lovely . . . Have you started it?"

HE: "Not yet. There's a gale blowing. Our pipes are broken, so there's no water. All I want to do is lie in bed and eat sweets. Can't sleep alone. I'm an old man already. Oh, yes, Happy New Year. 1903, imagine . . . I embrace you and kiss you, especially in my favorite place: the back of your neck. Such a soft little spot . . ."

SHE: "Couldn't sleep last night. Dark thoughts passed through my mind. I'm ashamed to call myself your wife. What have I given you?"

HE: "My sweetheart, you'll have children, you will, the doctors say so. No matter what, I shall find a way to be at your side; you'll have your little Grisha, a boy who will break your dishes and pull your dog's tail while you look on with pride . . ."

SHE: "Write to me about your health, Anton. I'm not there to care for you . . . It tortures me . . ."

HE: "My darling, believe me, if you were here, you'd be miserable. Be calm, my dearest, wait . . . and hope. Just hope . . ."

SHE: " 'We must live . . . We must live . . .' "

HE: "When I get better, let's go to Switzerland for two months! What do you say?"

SHE: "Switzerland? Wonderful! We'll be young again, like newlyweds."

HE: "When we go, I'll take nothing with me. Just an empty suitcase and my wife . . ."

SHE: "Are you writing?"

HE: "I'm trying . . . The temperature in my study is freezing. My man, Arseny, is a bit slow. He can't seem to heat it properly. Still, I manage to write a few lines a day. I'm very weak, and the cough . . ."

SHE: "Next year, you'll do as *I* say! You'll spend the whole winter here with me!"

HE: "March 18. My special heart: Work on the play is not going well. I'm a little blocked. So I'll come to Moscow in April, and after Easter, I'll be past it. I'll take you in my arms and kiss you forty-five times. Your Toto."

SHE: He came in April, but he didn't like our new flat. It was on the second floor, and took him half an hour to climb the stairs.

HE: We spent the whole summer together —

SHE: — but we had to return to Yalta. He was too unwell . . . And still no progress on the play . . . Then I left for Moscow, to start the new season . . .

HE: September 20, 1903. "Alone again in my hot Siberia. I spent all of last evening waiting for your telegram. How cruel, my darling. Write me news of the theater. I feel dried up as a dramatist. I'm so far away, I'm beginning to lose heart."

SHE: "My dearest, my precious fellow: What an awful train ride! That stupid Shaposhnikov, your friend, with his red hair and moustache — how I hate him! He kept fawning all over me, and then he'd take off his hat and cross himself every time we passed a church: 'For Chekhov's sake,' he kept saying. Unbearable! My darling, don't be sad! Go on writing, love each word, each thought, and realize how desperately people need them. Nemirovich is waiting, Stanislavsky is waiting . . . We're all waiting . . ."

HE: "Tell Stanislavksy I hope to finish the play next month. In the meantime, forgive me, darling. All I can manage is six or seven lines a day. I am trying so hard to write this play, really I am . . ."

SHE: "I'll be patience itself. Meanwhile, I'll send you a parcel tomorrow. I still can't find the right comb for your mother. I'm trying so hard to please her."

HE: "Our patience has been rewarded, little horsey. October 12: The play is finished. Tomorrow, I shall send it to Moscow. I'd have sent it earlier, but it took so long to copy. Tell me what you think. I don't know, I wrote it over such a long period of time . . . Today, we had mutton for lunch, which I can't eat any more. Porridge I can manage, and eggs . . . Oh, well, what does it matter, I won't lose heart. Don't worry, little dove. God be with you. I love you and will go on loving you forever. I might even beat you. I ought to take a mistress, but I haven't the energy . . . My darling, how difficult it was to write that play . . ."

SHE: When the script arrived, I crossed myself three times, and took it to the Art Theatre immediately. Stanislavsky snatched it from my hands. The next day, we read it aloud, and wept, how we wept. Stanislavsky telegrammed Anton, overwhelmed. "The most beautiful play you have written," he wired. "The author is a genius. I treasure every word. How we wept!"

HE: Wept? *Wept?* But it's a *comedy!*

SHE: A comedy? Really? But, my dearest —

HE: "A *comedy!* I cannot let Stanislasky ruin this play! . . . The doctors be damned. I'm coming to Moscow for rehearsals! And I *told* Stanislavsky to find an older actress for the company . . . But he didn't . . . So now *you'll* have to play the part of an old woman!"

SHE: Lyubov Andreevna? She's not an old woman! I'm overjoyed!

HE: And I've got to keep an eye on rehearsals . . . Oh, no — what about the stairs to the apartment?

SHE: My God, the lease . . . "I can't change apartments until March . . . I'll get a lift for you . . . And a new fur coat . . ."

HE: "I'll come by sleeping car. Bring my coat to the station — it will be cold."

SHE: "Anton, the doctors don't want you to come — and Stanislavsky is reluctant—"

HE: "I want to see my wife! Do I have a wife? Do I?"

SHE: "Talk to Dr. Altschuler and tell him it's imperative to come. Wire me. Kisses."

HE: "Coming Tuesday."

SHE: "Don't leave the train till I get there with your coat."

HE: "I'm coming, my darling . . . 'To Moscow!' "

(Music.)

SHE: It was as though fate, in that final year, bestowed upon him all that he loved: Moscow, a real Russian winter, *The Cherry Orchard*, and the people he cared for. Rehearsals were torture —"

HE: "A train in Act II? He wants a *train* in Act II? Stanislavsky must be stopped! . . . No crickets in Act II, either! He's ruining my play with these sound effects . . . And Act IV should be played in twelve minutes flat, not a moment more . . ."

SHE: He and Stanislavsky could not agree on anything, above all, on the tone —

HE: A drama?! The press release calls it a "drama"?!! It's a comedy! *The Cherry Orchard* is a *comedy!* . . . They don't understand my play!

SHE: Still, it was glorious. We premiered it on his forty-fourth birthday —

HE: January 17, 1904 . . .

SHE: They dragged him up on the stage at the end of Act III. A thunderous ovation. He was so weak he could hardly stand . . . "O my precious orchard, my sweet lovely orchard! . . . My life, my youth, my happiness, farewell! . . . Farewell . . ."

HE: "And life has passed by, somehow, as if I never lived it at all . . ."

(Music.)

SHE: In February, we went to Tsaritsyno to look for a small estate for the summer . . . On the way back, we drove by carriage for miles through the heaviest frost. How he loved it: the white plains glistening in the sun, the sound of the sleigh on the tightly packed snow . . . Fate spoiled him in those final months, giving him all the joys he'd longed for . . .

HE: "Hello, my darling! I'm on the boat back to Yalta, which leaves in three hours. I've got Schnapps with me. He's behaving just as he did on the train, barking at the ticket inspectors and feeling right at home. Now he's sitting on the deck, resting against my legs. He's forgotten all about Moscow! My sweetheart, I can't live without your letters. Write every day, or else divorce me . . . I think I hear Schnapps barking at someone down below. I'd better go and see . . ."

SHE: His last sojourn in Yalta . . . February, 1904 . . .

HE: "No word from you since I've returned, darling horsey. You're on tour in Petersburg, I know. Here, it's dreary and dull. I spend my time rereading last year's newspapers and old mail. Schnapps is either deaf or dumb. He simply won't go out of the house, and insists on spending the night in mother's room. He's extremely happy, but he's not very bright. I'm so lonely. You've spoiled me so that I've forgotten how to undress myself. Think I'll brush my teeth now. I'll go to the baths in May when I come to Moscow. In the meantime, I'll plant corn on my body; at least that way I'll make myself useful . . ."

SHE: "I found two apartments . . . One's on the second floor, but it has thirty-two steps and no lift. The other has a lift and there's a telephone under the stairs. Chaliapin lives there. What do you think?"

HE: "Take the second one . . . The sun hasn't shone since I've returned to Yalta. It's humid and grey, and I stay in my room. Where shall we spend the summer? I have such happy memories of Tsaritsyno. If you can find a dacha there, have a water closet installed. Tell them to run the pipes through the courtyard, dig a hole, cement it, and put in a pump. Get started on it soon. And in autumn — oh, never mind . . . dreams, only dreams . . . You have a cold! Shame on you for not wiring me: I worry so. Wire me about the dacha, too. It's what I live for . . ."

SHE: "It's a cold, nothing more . . .!"

HE: "I've heard about your raves in Petersburg. You've fallen out of love with me, my little star, haven't you? Admit it! I hear you might even divorce me! But then whom will you sleep with in the summer? Take care, my doggie — don't tire yourself. Today is Sunday, I took some powder — heroin — and I'm feeling very calm. I'm trying to write, but without much success. I have an idea for a play: a journey on a ship to the North Pole, with a woman and the ghost of her lover on board. But I don't have enough energy to start it yet. Tomorrow, perhaps . . ."

SHE: I know what —! "Let's give up the Moscow apartment and take a dacha in Tsaritsyno! What do you think?"

HE: "My darling little daschund: Only one month more and I'll come to Moscow. I can't stay here any more, I feel too ill, and there's nothing I can do about it, medicine or diet. Living without you, I'm next to nothing. The day is ended, thank God, no thoughts, no desires, just a game of patience, and pacing up and down. I dream of fishing, and wonder what I'll do with all the fish I've caught, only all I'll catch is one lone gudgeon with a death wish . . . Think of the man you married now and then . . . Your worthless one."

SHE: "Can you believe it, darling? We can rent a dacha in Tsaritsyno for 700 rubles a year! That's so cheap! What do you say?!"

HE: "My constant wife: Happy Easter! One or two more letters, and then this machine will stop. I'm leaving Yalta with the greatest of pleasure — I don't care if I ever return. It's dull here, there is no spring, and I don't feel well. I ran to the lavatory at least five times yesterday, though I hardly ate anything. I'm so short of breath. I cough constantly . . . Don't pine, little doggie. Remember I love you."

SHE: Anton? . . . You've stopped writing about the summer, about Tsaritsyno . . . What about our plans?

HE: "Sweetheart, I'm writing my last letter to you. Soon I'll be in Moscow. I felt awful yesterday, but today is better. All I eat now is eggs and soup. It's raining, the weather's dank and cold. Still, today, despite the rain, I went to the dentist . . . God bless you, my joy . . . You ask me: What is life? That is like asking: What is a carrot? A carrot is a carrot and that's all there is to it . . ."

SHE: His very last letter . . . April 22, 1904 . . . He came to Moscow at the end of the month, and immediately fell ill. Three weeks he lay in bed, suffering from great pain in all his muscles, especially in his legs. His digestive system was in ruins. Dr. Taube, who treated him, suggested he go to Badenweiler —

HE: Germany? God forbid!

SHE: There's a clinic there for chest diseases in the Black Forest. We could stay in a hotel, or a private apartment —

HE: Not a sanatorium — I refuse! . . . That would be the end . . .

SHE: We left for Berlin in June . . . I'll never forget his bewildered smile at the station, as we were leaving Russia. That smile left such a lasting impression on me . . . He wouldn't even let Masha and his mother see us off. In Berlin, more doctors, then south. In Badenweiler,

he improved at first, he could even walk around our hotel room —
he was breathless from the emphysema, though . . .

HE: We went for a drive almost every day . . . .

SHE: Dr. Schworer was gentle and friendly. Clearly, he knew Anton's
state was critical — everyone did — but he treated him with the
utmost kindness . . .

HE: He wasn't too bad to have around . . . *(Coughs.)*

SHE: We stayed in a private villa, where he could sit quietly in the
morning sun. He'd wait for the postman to bring letters and newspapers . . .

HE: The war with Japan . . . it's a tragedy . . . .

SHE: Then we moved again, to the Hotel Sommer, and a room flooded
with sunlight. He felt better. He spent hours in the garden, or sitting on the balcony, watching the provincial life of Badenweiler.

HE: "I'll need a white flannel suit for this society . . . How badly you
dress your husband, *mein leibchen . . .*"

SHE: "I can't order you a suit here!"

HE: "So go to Freiburg and order one! Don't worry, doggie, I'll be here
when you get back . . ."

SHE: The trip to Freiburg took a whole day. I hurried back, alarmed.

HE: "Ready in three days? That's all? Delightful!"

SHE: The morning of June 30 was hot. He returned from the garden
breathless, agitated —

HE: "We've got to find a room with windows facing north . . . I must see the forest . . ."

SHE: In two hours we were in our new room on the top floor, with a view over the mountains . . . That night was dreadful. It was hot and stormy. The air was stifling.

HE: "Open the door to the balcony . . ."

SHE: A thick white mist filled the room with filmy, fantastical shapes . . .

HE: "Turn the electric light off . . ."

SHE: It hurt his eyes . . . There was only one candle burning. I was terrified it wouldn't last till dawn. Clouds of mist floated everywhere . . . How unearthly it was with the candle sputtering, dying down, springing to life, dying down . . .

HE: "What are you reading? . . ."

SHE: I had taken a book and pretended to read . . . " 'The Black Monk,' darling . . . "

HE: "Silly little wife, taking her husband's stories on holiday!"

SHE: Once again, he slipped into oblivion. I put some ice on his heart, and he pushed it away —

HE: "An empty heart needs no ice . . ."

SHE: The next morning, he was better though. He even took some porridge . . .

HE: "Let me sit in the armchair by the window . . ."

SHE: At twilight, I went to the chemists for oxygen . . .

HE: "Go swim in the pool, darling, or take a walk in the park, get some air . . . You haven't been out of the room for days."

SHE: When I returned and saw his gentle, smiling face, I felt calmer. I missed the dinner bell, but a servant brought me something —

HE: "That reminds me of a story — do you know it? — about an exclusive spa where a group of spoiled Americans, after an exhausting day of sporting, greedily await a sumptuous meal —"

SHE: *(Laughs.)*

HE: "—only to discover, to their dismay, that the chef has run off with the headwaiter's wife! Imagine the reaction of all those pampered people!"

SHE: "Stop! It hurts to laugh . . ."

HE: "Remove the pillows from the bed, would you, my love?"

SHE: He lay down again, and smiled . . .

HE: "You see? I'm better today. Not so short of breath . . ."

SHE: At about one in the morning, he woke up.

HE: "The pain —"

SHE: He couldn't lie down, he was in such agony . . .

HE: "Call the doctor, please —"

SHE: It was the first time in his life he had asked for a doctor. But I took heart. Something would be done. Dr. Schworer came in, and sat down by the bed. He held Anton tenderly in his arms, and whispered something. Anton sat up suddenly and said loudly and clearly:

HE: "*Ich sterbe . . .*"

SHE: — though he knew no German. And then, he said:

HE: "*Shampanskoye, pozhaluste . . .*"

SHE: The doctor took a syringe, gave him an injection, and ordered champagne. When the champagne arrived, the doctor poured three glasses. He handed one to Anton and one to me. Anton looked at it, and smiled.

HE: "It's been such a long time since I drank champagne . . ."

SHE: He drank it, and lay quietly on his left side. I ran to the bed and leaned across it to comfort him, but he had already stopped breathing and lay there peacefully, like a sleeping child . . .

(Pause. LIGHTS down to half on HE.)

I sat up all night, beside the bed where he lay, waiting for them to come and prepare him, to take him back to Russia . . . Just before dawn — pow!!!— what was that?! The cork which the doctor had replaced in the champagne bottle — it flew right off! All of its own volition! The sound of it! . . . Just before dawn they came for him. The final journey. First back to Berlin, and then by train to Russia. Imagine, a coffin with his body in a train car marked "fresh oysters" — his favorite delicacy! Then into the Moscow station, with a small crowd awaiting him — Masha, his mother, his brothers, my family, and a procession through the streets to the Novodevichy, where the three sisters' mother was also buried . . .

(Pause.)

SHE: "We shall rest . . . we shall rest . . . we shall rest . . ."

(Lights down to one-quarter on HE. Music.)

SHE: August 19, 1904. Darling Anton: At last I am able to write to you, dearest, so near and yet so far! How strange it feels, and I know it's irrational, but I've had the desire to do so for weeks now. You were hurt I didn't write you this spring, while I was on tour in Petersburg. Forgive me, Anton, I'll make up for it now . . .

August 24. Five days since I've written, my darling, forgive me. Yesterday, I went back to the monastery with your brother, Misha. I bought a bench and had it placed at your graveside. How splendid it is! After the arid south everything here is so lush, so scented, the trees make a gentle, rustling sound . . .

August 27. Two days since I've written, but it seems like an eternity. I'm sitting at a rehearsal of *Ivanov* at the theater. It's dismal, they're performing like fools . . . I've spent some time in Yalta, darling. Masha has taken our bedroom. How angry she still is! Anton, I've tried so hard, really I have! But it was this way from the start. She always felt I was taking you from her. Why did it have to turn out this way?

August 30. Days pass, nights pass, can't tell the difference . . . That time in Yalta was so difficult, Anton. In the morning, when I awoke, there was no one in bed waiting for me with that sly, secretive look. Do you remember those mornings? I would kiss you, caress you. How grandly you would lie there. You told me jokes and made me laugh. Everything has withered in the garden. Arseny, that good-for-nothing, has disappeared. I wander about the almond orchard, and feel you walking beside me, your shoulder brushing my cheek.

September 11. Darling, it's been so long since I've written. I'm so disheveled, so distraught, you couldn't bear to see me. I want to kneel before you, lean my head against you, listen to your heartbeat. A few days before your death, we were talking and dreaming of Grisha, remember? He would have been two in November. Just think! How you would have loved him! The theater, the theater . . . I don't know whether to love it or to curse it. If only I'd given up the theater. Now it's all I have left. Forgive me . . . I take your hand in mine, my love . . . I hold your hand in mine . . . I kiss your hand hard . . .

HE: *(Lights come up on HE in blue.)* . . . and bow low, very low . . .

SHE: I kiss you and hug you, a thousand times . . . .

HE: . . . till my head touches the ground . . .

SHE: I love you, my gentle husband. . .

HE: I stroke your little shoulder . . .

SHE: I love you my poet . . .

HE: Remember me . . .

SHE: I kiss you and hold you . . .

HE: Remember me . . .

SHE: I wait for you . . .

HE: Remember me . . .

SHE: Come to me in my dreams. . .

HE: Remember me . . .

(Lights to half on both . . . then out.)

END OF PLAY

Olga Knipper, 1899. Of this photograph, Chekhov wrote: "Behind that expression of modest melancholy there lurks a little demon." (2/14/1900)

Anton Chekhov, Yalta, 1900.

Anton Chekhov and Olga Knipper on their honeymoon in Aksyonovo, 1901.
Chekhov wrote: "In this photograph, you look like a little German, a sweet and gentle
wife of a doctor — the kind who has no practice, that is . . ." (11/11/1901)

The Chekhov family, 1902.
From bottom left, clockwise: Yevgenia Chekhov (mother), Masha Chekhov (sister), Olga Knipper, and Chekhov.

Olga Knipper and Anton Chekhov, 1902.

Pronunciation Guide

Note: Accentuated syllable is highlighted

Alush	A-**loosh**
Anton Pavlovich	**An**-ton **Pav**-lo-veech
Arkadina	Ar-**ka**-dee-na
Arseny	Ar-**syeh**-nee
Badenweiler	**Ba**-den-veye-ler ("veye" rhymes with "my") (German)
Chaliapin	Cha-**lya**-peen
dacha	**da**-cha
decolleté	de-co-le-**tay** (French)
Dyoma	**Dyo**-ma
golubchik	go-**loob**-cheek
Grisha	**Gree**-sha
"ich sterbe"	ikh **shter**-beh ("I am dying" in German)
Knippusha	**Kni**-poo-sha
Knipperschitz	**Kni**-per-schitz
Kontan	Kon-**tan**
krilolinchik	kree-no-**leen**-cheek

Kuprin	Koo-**preen**
Levitan	Lyeh-vee-**tan**
Lombat	Lom-**bat**
Lyubimovka	Lyu-**bee**-mov-ka
Lyubov Andreevna	Lyoo-**bov** An-**drye**-yev-na
Melikhovo	**Myeh**-lee-kho-vo
Nemirovich	Neh-mee-**ro**-veech
Novodevichy	No-vo-**dyeh**-vee-chee
"pozhaluste"	po-**zha**-loo-steh ("please" in Russian)
"shampanskoye"	sham-**pan**-sko-yeh ("champagne" in Russian)
Shaposhnikov	Sha-**posh**-nee-kof
Stanislavsky	Sta-nee-**slav**-skee
Tolstoy	Tol-**stoy**
Tsaritsyno	Tsa-**ree**-tsee-no
Vishnievsky	Veesh-**nyev**-skee

Notes from the Playwright/Translator

Throughout the play, the actor and actress segue from the letters and the dialogue into segments of scenes of the four major plays of Anton Chekhov.

For the actors performing these parts, it is helpful to know that the dialogue from the four plays included in "*I take your hand in mine . . .*" is as follows:

p. 3–4   From *The Seagull,* Act III, scene between Arkadina and Trigorin

p. 6–7   From *Uncle Vanya,* Act IV, scene between Yelena and Astrov

p. 7   From *The Seagull,* Act IV, Nina's line in the scene between Nina and Treplev

p. 14   From *The Three Sisters,* Masha's lines in Act IV in the scene with Chebutykin, and in Act I (the ensemble scene)

p. 15–16 From *The Three Sisters,* Act III, Masha's confession to Olga and Irina

p. 18   From *The Seagull,* Act I, Trigorin's line in the ensemble scene

p. 22   From *The Three Sisters,* Act II, Irina's final lines

p. 32   From *Uncle Vanya,* Act IV, Sonya's final speech

p. 35   From *The Cherry Orchard,* Act IV, Lyubov Andreevna's line in the final scene with Gaev

Please note that the excerpts of all these scenes from the major plays, as well as from the letters and memoirs, have been translated by the author of this play from the original Russian sources. Complete translations of these plays can be found in *Chekhov: Four Plays.* Translated by Carol Rocamora. 1996, Smith & Kraus.

Bibliography

The following are the original sources from which the letters of Anton Chekhov and the letters and memoirs of Olga Knipper have been translated for "*I take your hand in mine . . .*" by the playwright:

Chekhov, Anton. *Polnoe Sobranie Sochineniy i Pisem v tridtsati tomax.* Moscow, Izdatelstvo 'Nauka', 1974–82.

Knipper-Chekhova, Olga Leonardovna. *Vospominania i Stati. Perepiska s A. P. Chekhovim.* Moskva, Izdatelstvo "Iskustvo," 1972.

Perepiska A. P. Chekhova i O. L. Knipper (v dvyx tomax). Moskva, Kooperativnoe Izdatelstvo, 1934.

The following are sources for biographical detail:

Rayfield, Donald. *Anton Chekhov: A Life.* New York: Henry Holt and Company, 1997.

Simmons, Ernest J. *Chekhov: A Biography.* University of Chicago Press, 1962.

Troyat, Henri. *Chekhov.* New York: Fawcett Colombine, 1986.

The following is the source for quotations from the plays of Anton Chekhov:

Chekhov: Four Plays. Translated by Carol Rocamora. Lyme, N.H.: Smith and Kraus, 1996.

Acknowledgments

Special thanks to Olympia Dukakis and Louis Zorich for their reading at the Tisch School of the Arts of New York University in December, 1999. Heartfelt thanks also to Terry Zaroff and Eric Parillo, and to Karen McDonald and John Rothman, for their respective readings at the Vineyard Playhouse in July, 1999 and August, 2000. Thanks to Kate Davis for musical accompaniment, and to M. J. Munafo and Jon Lipsky for their hospitality. Also, appreciation to Jennifer Camp for editorial assistance.

The Author

Carol Rocamora, translator, director, teacher, and playwright, is a graduate of Bryn Mawr College. She received her M. A. and Ph. D. degrees from the University of Pennsylvania in Russian literature.

She is the founder of the Philadelphia Festival Theatre for New Plays at the Annenberg Center, a non-profit professional theatre, where she served as Artistic and Producing Director from 1981–1994. At the Annenberg Center, she directed many mainstage productions, including the premieres of her four new translations of Chekhov's major plays.

Dr. Rocamora's translations of Chekhov's complete dramatic works have been recently published by Smith and Kraus. The publications are: *Chekhov: Four Plays* (*The Seagull, Uncle Vanya, The Three Sisters, The Cherry Orchard*) (1996); *Chekhov: The Vaudevilles* (1998): and *Chekhov: The Early Plays* (*Platonov, Ivanov, The Wood Demon*) (1999).

Dr. Rocamora has served on the faculties of Bryn Mawr and Haverford Colleges, and the University of Pennsylvania. She currently teaches theatre in the Department of Dramatic Writing at New York University's Tisch School of the Arts.